The Art of
Process
Improvement

ABDUL A JALUDI

DEDICATION

This work is dedicated to my wife Stefanie, whom I love deeply, and who stood by patiently while I was off on one project after another and to my children Joey, Mandy and Dylan who grew up while I was away, yet managed to become my proudest accomplishments.

Contents

Introduction 1

About the author 4

1. Corporate Foundation.................................... 7

2. Process Management...................................... 13

3. Assessment 17

4. Preparation 21

5. Formulation... 25

6. Standards and Processes............................... 28

7. Engagement 32

8. Adapting.. 36

9. Implementation 39

10. Resources 46

11. Environment... 50

12. Drastic Action 58

13. Prep work and information gathering 62

14. Bibliography 67

THE ART OF PROCESS IMPROVEMENT

INTRODUCTION

The Art of Process Improvement is a high level strategic book aimed at helping companies better compete by improving productivity, reducing expenses and improving employee morale using principles outlined in one of the greatest war strategy books ever written, The Art of War by Sun Tzu.

The Art of War by Sun Tzu is not a book on how to fight during a battle, but rather a guide for steps to follow or avoid when developing the war strategy. The Art of Process Improvement is much the same. It will not teach how to evaluate or re-engineer a process but rather the steps to follow or avoid when attempting to do so.

The term 'continual process improvement' is somewhat redundant. Process improvement is not something you do once then walk away. As demands, needs, conditions and technology change, the process you just re-engineered needs to evolve as well.

In times of economic crisis, many companies cut expenses to deal with the crisis by reducing staff. This approach provides an immediate short term relief, but at the cost of employee morale. The remaining staff as a result is forced to work additional hours to make up for the lost help, usually with no increase, and in some cases, a reduction of total compensation.

Other companies keep staffing levels the same, but cut expenses elsewhere, either through benefit reductions, travel and other expense cutbacks, inventory reductions and so on. This approach backfires when the crisis lingers. Productivity is down, since there is less demand for the company's products, while staffing levels are still at pre-crisis levels. Employee morale also drops as many workers feel unproductive, not helping contribute to the bottom line as much as they feel they should. To make matters worse, everyone is keenly aware that staffing cuts are just around the corner.

Companies which weather the crisis the best, lead the pack during good and bad times, are the ones which continually look at and refine how work is done. These companies have ingrained the practice of process improvements into the culture of the company.

Rather than bleeding a company quickly as in the first approach or slowly as in the second, companies which employ a process improvement philosophy stand out above the rest, are usually well known within the industry as leaders and endure for generations. Some of these are McDonald's, Wal-Mart, Honda, Nestlé and a host of many others.

These companies don't have to make any changes, as they are already efficient, well managed and continually adjust to market conditions as a normal business practice. These companies have a clear goal, which every employee understands and strives for as well as a process in place to continually adapt to changing conditions. In other words these companies practice and have become adept at the art of process improvement.

ABOUT THE AUTHOR

Having had twenty-five years experience with process improvement in the financial services industry, Abdul Jaludi has espoused and championed *efficiency* as a crucial element in successfully and consistently meeting customer's needs and expectations. Facilitating twenty-four-seven stability and availability within the unforgiving business environs of intense competitive pressure and strict regulatory requirements has been an ever-changing trial throughout his tenure. It is nevertheless within these challenging and high-stakes environs that Jaludi has been able to help establish one of the most efficient mainframe banking environments in the world – leading innovation in procedure automation; and department, function, process and tool optimization – well before such improvements were thought practical, or even possible.

His firsthand experience has enabled Jaludi to fully understand and embrace how process improvement, change management, and corporate culture are critical factors in determining how an organization can efficiently address and react to rapid changes in the business environment. The lessons learned during those twenty-five years are the genesis of this book, which focuses on the concept of process improvement, how to implement change and innovation, and the role of leadership in making these crucial elements of success an integral part of the corporate culture.

1. CORPORATE FOUNDATION

1. The art of process improvement is vital to the health of the Company. The success or failure of the company depends on it being woven into the culture of the company.

2. The art of successful process improvement, then, is guided by five constant factors, to be taken into account when seeking to determine its effectiveness. These are:

   a) Goal

   b) Business environment

   c) Competition

   d) Leadership

   e) Employee morale and discipline

The successful leader should be thoroughly familiar in each of these five. Omit one and you are doomed to fail.

3. Goal: the Company should have a clear goal that every employee knows, understands and strives towards. Improvements must lead towards the goal.

4. Business environment: understand market and economic conditions and be prepared for changes in either direction. Know which improvements to seek for each condition.

5. Competition: be aware of your competitors, their strategy, movements and all improvements they are undertaking

6. Leadership: Ensure you have strong loyal leaders who understand the importance of continual improvement. Strong leaders must have all of the following five virtues:

    a) Wisdom – ability to plan and to know when to change effectively. Reliance on wisdom alone results in rebelliousness

    b) Trustworthy – use rewards and punishments to ensure loyalty. Relying on trust alone without rewards and punishments will lead to deceit

c) Benevolence – compassion and understanding towards people and the problems they face. Too much compassion will lead to weakness and indecisiveness

d) Courage – ability to seize an opportunity without delay. Too much courage will lead to excessive risk taking

e) Strictness – ability to establish discipline by enforcing rules, policies and taking disciplinary actions. Excessive rules and wanton disciplinary actions are cruel and will lead to abandonment and revolts

To succeed and cultivate a culture of continual improvement, a leader must achieve harmony with these five traits.

7. Employee morale and discipline: ensure a program to reward, punish and train is in place. In order for employees to know and strive for the goal, they must be loyal and given tools and the opportunity to contribute towards continuous improvements.

8. The leader that can achieve harmony with these five disciplines will prosper. Leaders that preach but do not understand and practice all of them will not succeed.

9. When comparing companies, those that practice these disciplines will be a better long term investment.

    a) Which company has a clearly defined goal understood and followed by all?

    b) Which company is prepared for changes in demand or market conditions?

    c) Which company knows and reacts to what its competition is doing?

    d) Which company has a strong leader that:

        i. Has the hearts of the workers

        ii. Is fair and ensures corporate policy is applied equally across the board

    e) Which company has the loyalty of the workers:

        i. A level of trust and fairness exists between Management and staff

        ii. Low staff turnover

    f) Which company is more productive:

        i. Has better policies, procedures and tools

    g) Which company applies corporate policy equally across the board?

        i. Everyone, low level worker through senior executive, are treated alike: when improvements are productive, rewards the workers and management. When productive improvements do not materialize, both are equally punished

ii. Rewards are not out of proportion among differing levels

iii. Punishments are not arbitrary

10. By examining these seven, the better company will be known.

11. The leader who heeds and practices this advice will prosper and become a great leader. The one who fails to follow this advice will see failure and dismissal.

12. Examine current conditions and engage all affected parties before trying to develop a plan. Adjust your plan then allocate your resources based on feedback and strategic direction.

13. When engaging users for feedback, don't appear to know more than the users. If you know the process, act as if you don't and allow them to tell you; you might have missed something. If you have a solution that will work, act as if you don't and lead them to reach one; they may reach the same solution or a better one.

a) Users will be more likely to help you

b) Users will feel like they are part of the solution and more likely to help implement the solution

c) If you appear knowing the problem and the solution, they will see you as being arrogant, out of touch and will be less likely to provide their support

14. When looking at a process improvement that will reduce labor requirements, hide your true intent from the management of that group. These are usually empire builders who will attempt to obstruct you.

15. Gain their confidence with the prospect of more resources, and then get access to their staff.

16. Be alert and wary when facing someone full of knowledge. Avoid someone who makes up facts, wait for someone with factual knowledge.

17. Anger your opponents by remaining calm and clear headed; they will not think clearly and will lose credibility.

2. PROCESS MANAGEMENT

1. A full scale process improvement project with a large team is very expensive.

2. Do not spend all your time analyzing.

3. Analyze too much and you will lose sight of your goal.

4. Others will come up with a solution in the meantime.

5. Over analysis will derail the task
   a) Better to find a partial improvement then to look forever for a complete solution

6. One must weigh the time factor against the need before proceeding.

    a) It is important to know what is more important

        i. A partial solution now

        ii. A complete solution in the distant future

7. Implement partial solutions that will lead to your goal

    a) Avoid solutions that are just a quick fix and lead nowhere

    b) Partial solutions should be stepping stones to a complete solution

8. Do not waste time on complicated and expensive tools. Where possible:

    a) Use what is available at hand

    b) Customize what is there to meet needs

9. Avoid using already overworked staff for your project

    a) Normal work will suffer and your project may be terminated

    b) Service delivery levels should improve, not diminish during this process

10. A few will attempt to take credit for the work of others

    a) Give credit where due and when due

    b) Allow everyone a chance to be heard

        i. Some will give you overly complicated solutions

        ii. Others may have a good solution but were unable to present it

11. Analyze too much and your budget will be drained before your solution is ready.

12. Find a solution where the net save or gain will be more than the expense to implement and operate.

13. Staff that are unhappy with the current process will be more inclined to help replace it

    a) Recognition for helping with the improvement will motivate them

14. Provide awards for the first to help

    a) Others will be motivated

15. Treat staff who oppose the process well and as equals

    a) They may in time support you

16. This will lead to less resistance and additional sources for information, ideas and aid to the project team.

17. The important thing to remember is to show actual progress rather than visions of progress.

18. The leader managing the project holds the advancement or downfall of the team, department, division or entire company.

3. ASSESSMENT

1. It is better to implement an optimized process the first time than to go back and rework it.

2. Continually improving the same process is counterproductive. The real gains are made by creating processes that need no immediate improvement.

3. The goal should be to optimize a process while it is being developed.

4. The next best is to find improvements while the process is in the pilot stage.

5. The next best is to find improvements in the process when it is already in use.

6. The lowest option is to look for improvements in staffing rather than the process.

   a) This should be the last resort, after the process has been optimized

7. Enough time should be taken to allow for full understanding of the problems with the current process and to formulate the improvement strategy.

8. Don't utilize the vast majority of your budget in trying to understand the problems with the current process and formulating your recommendations.

   a) Budget money will be needed to develop and implement your solution

9. One who is good at analysis should be able to understand the problems and formulate recommendations shortly after seeing the current process.

10. The best improvements are found and implemented without much delay using existing resources.

11. If you have endless resources, simply bring in a better process to replace the current one. If your resources are fairly large, use them to compare which would be more cost effective, a replacement or finding and implementing improvements. If your

resources are limited, use them to identify the issue then formulate and implement the improvements.

12. When confronting resistance, stand your ground if you can win your case and make progress. If you cannot win, don't argue. If resistance is from senior managers, avoid the confrontation altogether.

13. You will waste your entire budget if you continue when faced with strong resistance by senior management within the current process owners.

14. Process analysts exist for the benefit of the company. Without process optimization, the company will falter.

15. Management can derail the process improvement by implementing an improvement without knowing the ramifications, moving to the development stage before the analysis is completed, by instructing the analyst on what improvements to make without knowing the process flow fully. This is equivalent to sabotage.

    a) To succeed, the analyst will need to be autonomous

16. There are five ways of knowing who will succeed in a process improvement initiative:

a) Those who know when to confront management and when to stand back

b) Those who know when to use part or all of their budget

c) Those who are fully supported by staff and management

d) Those who take the time to fully understand the current process and the reason for change

e) Those who are able to make decisions based on analysis rather than management dictate

17. When performing a process improvement project:

a) If you are confident in your abilities and know the issues, you will find the optimal process a hundred times in a row.

b) If you are confident in your abilities, but do not fully understand the issues, you will find the optimal process one out of two times

c) If you do not have confidence in yourself, and do not fully understand the issues, you will never find the optimal process

4. PREPARATION

1. Be prepared. Know your subject inside and out. Find out what the others do not know and use it against them to make your point. Know more than the person you will be confronting.

2. It is up to you to be fully prepared with all the details of the current process and the issues at hand. Let the other be unprepared rather than you.

3. Getting fully prepared and knowledgeable does not mean that the others opposing you are less so, they may be just as prepared as you.

4. Based on your preparations, success may be foretold accurately, but when both sides are fully prepared, success may not materialize.

5. Those who are prepared will defend their points, those who aren't will brag about their success.

6. When you are unsure of the facts keep a low profile. When you have all the facts pounce while they are not expecting it.

   a) Complete the task before providing any indication of your status lest anyone tries to block it before you've finished

   b) While collecting your information, keep what you have collected private. Present your case only when you have collected all of your information and formulated a strategy

7. Take advantage of your strengths. If your strength is analysis, dig deeply into the problem. If your strength is debate, let someone else do the analysis and you persuade to implement.

8. Improving a broken process is not really a skill. Be careful what you call a victory.

9. Don't brag about the obvious.

10. Those that fix obviously broken processes are not really experts in the field.

11. The ones that constantly fix these issues are not known for good analytical skills. The improvements they make are not things that are stumbled upon. They were able to make the easy improvements by knowing and hiding the underlying issues. The skilled analyst will turn the hardest issue into a simple process improvement.

12. A good analyst will have full backing from management senior enough to ensure department cooperation before proceeding. They do not overlook matters where it will be easy to shutdown the project from the department being analyzed.

13. A successful analyst will have all of his support before starting his project. A poor analyst will begin his project then attempt to get management backing.

14. Those who have a formalized process can dictate direction. They can go into any project and succeed over a management that is disorganized or corrupt.

15. There are five rules of analysis:

    a) Assessment of the project

    b) Analysis of the issues

    c) Formulation of a solution

    d) Comparison of possible solutions

e) Implementation of solution

16. A successful analyst will have the force of the entire company. A mediocre analyst will be alone. When the successful analyst begins a project, it is like watching a work of art. It is a thing of beauty when everyone knows exactly what to do.

5. FORMULATION

1. Managing a large process improvement is a matter of looking at the smaller pieces that make up the entire process.

2. Performing successful process improvements means sometimes thinking outside the box. Be willing to look at any option, not just the standard practices.

3. For the analyst to make the most difficult problem look like a simple puzzle is a matter of simplicity and innovation.

4. When analyzing, facing the problem head on will lead to confrontations. The analysis will succeed when brought on quickly and unexpectedly.

5. Those who explore all options, the proven and the innovative, will build up a reputation for success.

6. When mixing proven methods with new innovations, the things that can be analyzed and improved are endless.

7. When the speed of rushing water reaches the point where it can move boulders, this is the force of momentum. When the speed of a hawk is such that it can strike and kill, this is precision. So it is with the skilled analysts. Their analysis is swift, their solution on the mark. Their analysis is like an avalanche, their solution is like the precision of a rocket.

8. Analyst solutions that are the most effective

    a) Are willingly followed

    b) Lead naysayers into a false sense of security, letting the new process take form before they can object

9. Analysts that are most effective are given more opportunities as a result of their record. They are able to choose people and let the force of their momentum do its part in their work.

10. Getting people to work on a project by using momentum is like rolling logs and rocks. Logs and

rocks are still when in a secure place, but roll on an incline; they remain stationary if square, they roll if round. Therefore, when people are skillfully managed on a project, the momentum is like that of round rocks rolling down a high mountain.

6. STANDARDS AND PROCESSES

1. Those who are prepared, first on site and ready to begin, are at ease. Those who come late and are unprepared, will get exhausted trying to keep up.

2. Those with defined standards and processes will be at ease with any task.

3. Those without, will be lost and will have difficulty repeating even the same task.

4. An expert analyst will define the new process rather than have it told to him.

5. What makes management come to you is the prospect of success. What discourages management from coming to you is the prospect of failure.

6. Take on what your team can handle comfortably.

   a) Too many projects at one time mean they will all be delayed.

   b) Not enough projects causes distraction and laziness.

7. The skilled leader eliminates resistance to the project before proceeding.

8. Your chances for success are greater if you implement in areas where there is least resistance.

9. Your project becomes stronger when others have no arguments they can make against it.

10. Consequently, the skilled leader is the one who asks unexpected questions to those opposing the project and has the proper answers to any questions they pose.

11. There is an advantage in only providing minimal information and holding back the rest.

12. Implement your changes in areas with no resistance in a timely manner.

13. If the project needs to move forward but there is resistance, distract those who would oppose with other critical workloads.

14. If the project is not in a position to move forward, avoid confrontation by giving those who oppose an unexpected workload or deliverable.

15. Knowing the department's arguments without revealing your information keeps your team united while your opposition must remain divided.

16. If there is a debate as to the merits of the project, you will be in the stronger position.

17. Adding bodies to a project will not necessarily guarantee success.

18. Be willing to adapt to the project at hand. Presenting one case to win a different one will lead to failure if they are not compatible type projects.

19. Knowing the answers to all possible arguments will strengthen your position.

20. Keeping your strategy secret will enhance your chances for success.

21. Success depends on how well you can adapt to the current project and environment.

22. Everyone will know your argument when you make it, but none will know as you are preparing it.

23. There is no standard model for undertaking a process improvement project. The only standard is to adapt to the requirements of each project.

7. ENGAGEMENT

1. The detailed analysis starts after the initial review determines that no other option exists.

2. The work starts only when the most senior of management gives the signal to all, since nothing is more difficult than working with a hostile team.

3. The difficulty of facing a hostile department is using the hostility to circumnavigate stubborn workers and turning problems into opportunities.

4. Consequently you make their job even more difficult by luring them with hopes of slowing your progress. When you keep them occupied this way, you get around them to find the real problems.

5. Their hostility blinds them to what your actual intents are and allows you to move unhindered.

6. Letting the project linger on for too long will derail the project. As the duration increases, the chances for success decrease.

7. If you don't know what the workers are doing, you will not be able to make informed decisions.

8. Unless you know all of the procedures, processes and workflows, your analysis will stall without guidance from someone within the current department.

9. The detailed analysis is planned through deception, started by small gains, and continued through division of the hostile team.

10. Consequently when the analysis begins it is like the flowing river; when it performs in-depth analysis it is like a sponge; it becomes as unstoppable as lightning.

11. The movement of the analysis continues unabated.

12. Act when the analysis is complete. The ones who know when to finish come out ahead.

13. Use certain aspects of your analysis to ensure your entire team is on board with the entire assessment. One may see gain within one area while another will see gain elsewhere.

14. Use the same strategy to win the hearts of the department workers and weaken the resistance of their management.

15. Avoid confrontation in the morning when everyone is keen and alert. Best to approach during mid-day or later.

16. Use calmness to quell discontent and the rowdy.

17. Stand your ground and let the uninformed try to argue against you rather than the other way around.

18. Avoid the confrontation if they are well organized and ready to argue.

19. The rule is not to attempt an impossible analysis or to argue with those who have nothing to lose.

20. Don't get drawn into showing your hand to a seemingly friendly, hostile department.

21. Watch out for miss-information.

22. When they finally give in, let them leave in peace if they wish.

23. Don't take away everything from them with nothing to show for their contribution to the company. There must be some incentive for them to stay through the project completion.

24. Don't press employees who have nothing left to lose.

8. ADAPTING

1. Normally, the request to perform the analysis comes from outside the group.

2. The analyst needs to adapt to the current situation. When everyone is fighting fires, sit tight and wait, when there is calm, or what is normal for the environment, proceed.

3. There may be departments, groups or times where the analysis shouldn't be done despite the orders given.

4. Consequently analysts who can adapt to every possible situation know how to optimize. Analysts, who do not know how to adapt, even if they are experts at process improvement, cannot take advantage of the situation. If they proceed with the

analysis without adapting, they may not get the support of those they need.

5. Consequently the smart analyst will always consider both benefits and issues. As they see benefits, their work can progress, as they confront issues, any problems can be resolved.

6. Consequently, what holds back detractors are issues, what keeps detractors busy is work, what motivates them is profit and recognition.

7. So, the rule for process analysis is not to count on detractors not being there, but to rely on having ways of dealing with them; not to count on detractors laying interference, but on having what can't be interfered with.

8. Consequently there are five traits that are dangerous in a process analysis team leader:

   a) Those who are stubborn, thoughtless and reckless can lead to the elimination of the team

   b) Those who try to please everyone will please no one

   c) Those who are quick to lose their temper can be lured into using slander and disgrace

   d) Those who claim to be above everyone else can be disgraced

e)   Those who are too emotional and over protective of their staff will have trouble continuing or doing a proper analysis

9. These five are not quality characteristics of a leader, and disaster for a process improvement project.

10. When a process improvement team gets disbanded, it will usually be due to one of these traits.

9. IMPLEMENTATION

1. When you station someone to observe the workers, avoid the ones who talk rather than work and stay with those who perform the most work.

2. When they break, go with them, when they are engaged in difficult work, analyze but don't bother them. Wait till work slows to begin engaging them.

3. When faced with stiff resistance, don't cross over to their side to try persuading them. It is easier to let them get interested first then try to persuade them.

4. When you are ready to implement a new process, start where you have acceptance rather than where there is resistance.

5. Go through any resistance as quickly as possible without hesitation, ensuring you have senior management backing.

6. When all things are equal during implementation, start where it is easiest to implement and expand from there.

7. By following the last four steps the most difficult of improvements can be implemented.

8. The ideal process improvements are implemented under the visibility and support of senior management, and hardest to do when there is no senior management support and oversight.

9. Ensure you have management oversight and enough resources to implement.

10. When there is resistance or roadblocks engage the change management teams to keep them in check. An advantage to the process improvement is getting the Change Management teams on your side.

11. If there is a crisis happening in the department, wait till things settle before proceeding.

12. When the implementation is underway, if you keep hitting obstacles while everything appears normal, be on the lookout for saboteurs. You may also have spies ready to raise any issues found to senior management.

13. When detractors are close but quiet, they are on watch sensing opportunity. When they are making noise and causing hostilities, they want you to proceed quickly hoping you make mistakes. If they are making the disturbances themselves, then they've found an advantageous argument.

14. When e-mails and documents start flowing to management, the detractors are coming out into the open. When there is just noise within the department, they are trying to derail the project through confusion.

15. If rumors start spreading someone is plotting. If the hardest of workers become worried, get prepared to face stiff opposition. If the noise is internal and low within the groups, the resistance is with the staff; if it is in the open with e-mails and phone calls the resistance is with the department management. E-mails and information going from staff to department management indicate they are collecting data. E-mails from department management to seniors indicate they have enough data to stop the project.

16. Those who say little while collecting harmful data are going to make progress against you. Those who are noisy while trying to stop you have nothing to back them up and will stop when confronted.

17. When low level managers observe from the sidelines, they are setting up positions to watch for any opportunity to block the project.

18. Those who come to offer to help without any gain or advantage without being asked are there to plot.

19. When management suddenly starts appearing alongside the low level managers, they are expecting a senior manager to step in. Be prepared with any arguments which they may have for stopping the project.

20. If half of the department start attacking while the other half backs off, they are trying to get you to make mistakes.

21. If they stop fighting you, they've been disconnected from their management. When the first ones to communicate with their management begin arguing, they've run out of valid reasons to continue against you.

22. When they see mistakes and issues without reporting them, they no longer oppose the project.

23. When the rumors start again, the low level managers have returned back to their normal work.

24. When they keep calling department managers at all hours, the low level managers are nervous, fearing the department managers are too scared to show themselves.

25. If the workers and low level managers are nervous, it means the department managers are losing authority and fearful over their jobs.

26. If normal procedures are no longer followed, there is confusion in the ranks.

27. If they are irritable, they are tired of fighting.

28. When there are no other jobs, they will become desperate to keep the ones they have.

29. When there are lapses in duties and more water cooler conversations, the groups' loyalty to current management has been lost.

30. When they start handing out additional and unwarranted praise and rewards it means they are grasping at straws. When they start giving out additional and unwarranted punishments and reprimands, they are desperate and worn out.

31. Objecting loudly at first, then to end up afraid of your own staff, is the sign of incompetence.

32. Those who become humble have lost momentum and support.

33. When they are firm yet do nothing, be careful, something is up.

34. When implementing, adding resources is not always the best move; it is usually enough to leverage existing resources.

35. The person who works alone without a plan and makes light of existing processes will end up the pawn or sacrificial lamb.

36. If workers are punished before you have their loyalty, they will become harder to discipline and manage.

37. If workers aren't punished when doing wrong after you have their loyalty, they will become arrogant and unproductive.

38. Be benevolent and rewarding when warranted, and stern and punishing where required to guarantee loyalty, dedication and hard work.

39. Always be consistent when issuing rewards or punishments to everyone alike. When everyone is treated equally there will be greater harmony between workers and management.

10. RESOURCES

1. Some procedures and process are easy to follow, some are hard and some almost impossible. When work is getting done on a regular and timely basis, the process is easy to follow.

    a) Those who recognize the type of process before proceeding gain an advantage

2. Diving headstrong, without understanding the environment, and failing, due to not understanding the process, is the fault of the leader.

3. Having insufficient resources to complete the project, will lead to failure.

4. Bringing a large group when only one or two are needed, will lead the project towards failure.

5. When the workers start leading the project rather than the leader, the project will fail.

6. Having a strong leader but weak staff is another sign of pending failure.

7. Weak leaders who don't lead with authority and clear direction will result in insubordination and staff losing focus.

8. Staff members who get emotional perform miscellaneous tasks unrelated to the project, further deteriorating the chances for success.

9. Leaders who are unable to assess the current environment and project, spend time arguing with department managers, and have not properly assessed their teams talent, are headed towards failure.

10. These six are sure signs of pending project failure:

    a) Failure to properly assess needed resources

    b) Showing favoritism when assigning work or when handing out rewards and punishments

    c) Improperly train or prepare staff

    d) Overly emotional and working aimlessly or beginning too soon

    e) Lack of authority and clear direction

f) Failure to assess (or improperly assessing) workers' skills

11. These are ways a project can fail. The leader who knows these and avoids them is more likely to succeed and advance.

12. Properly assessing and adapting to the environment and existing processes is a pre-requisite. Those who begin without a proper assessment or cannot adapt to the current environment will fail.

13. Corporate policy and management support is the leader's strongest ally, but the ability to understand the requirements, examine the benefits and pitfalls, properly determine and control resistance and resources is the true test of a strong leader.

14. The leader who not only knows these things but puts them into practice will successfully complete projects on time, those who don't put them into practice will fail or continually miss key milestones.

15. Continuing or stopping despite managements objections is sometimes required when it means significant improvement or when the project is headed for certain failure.

16. The leader who completes projects for the benefit of the improvement without seeking glory or terminates them when the desired outcome is not achievable without hiding it is one of the greatest assets of the company.

17. Treat your staff as children and they will work hard, treat them as favorite sons and daughters and they will work even harder for you.

18. If you become too friendly with them that you can't give them tough assignments or discipline them they become spoiled and useless.

19. If you know your staff but not the requirements at hand, you have half a chance of success. If you know the requirements but not the capabilities of your staff, you have half a chance of success. If you know the requirements and the capabilities of the staff but unsure of the climate for change, you have half a chance for success.

20. If you know your abilities and the current requirements, your chances for success are good. When you know the capabilities of the staff, the current requirements, the environment and the climate for change, your chances for success are great.

11. ENVIRONMENT

1. Learn to recognize the different environments

    a) Your own department

    b) Defensive departments

    c) Open departments who will follow anyone

    d) Departments with no resistance

    e) Departments with matrix reporting lines

    f) Departments with overly onerous processes and requirements

    g) Departments with excessive paperwork, and follow up requirements

    h) Departments with complicated audit and compliance requirements

    i) Departments with no chance of success

2. Consequently

    a) Within your own department, cause no disruption but proceed with a watchful eye on distractions

    b) With defensive departments, don't delay but move quickly

    c) With open departments, avoid unneeded arguments

    d) In areas with no resistance, proceed carefully and watch for others with a similar goal

    e) In areas with matrix management, garner support from senior management along both lines of business before proceeding

    f) In areas with onerous processes, dispose of complicated rules and requirements which serve no purpose

    g) In areas with excessive paperwork and follow up, show progress as the project moves along

    h) In areas with complicated audit and compliance requirements, wade through the process to determine which are valid and which are just obstacles that can be discarded

    i) In areas with no chance of success, reorganize the department

3. The good process improvement leader is the one who can garner support from the staff despite department management's opposition.

4. When the entire department is against the project, he/she can convince the staff it is to their benefit.

5. Knows when the advantage is to move forward or pause.

6. When confronted with a large organized team of resistance, take away what they want most to make them listen to you.

7. The essential element for the process improvement team is speed, taking advantage of an opportune moment before resistance sets in.

8. As the process improvement project gains momentum, it becomes harder to stop, the process improvement team becomes more motivated.

9. When the processes are properly documented, let your team members learn as much as they can. Don't over extend or stress your team. Document what is learned in a central knowledge database.

10. Teams work best when they fear delay may lead to an endless situation. If they can't leave until the work is completed, they will work hard.

11. Under these conditions the team members will be fully motivated, produce good results in a timely manner without requiring constant oversight.

12. If the team members have too many things to worry about, personal or professional, they will be distracted and less productive.

13. A successful process improvement project is prepared with persons who can speak regarding: benefits, problems, staffing, compliance, budgeting resources and so on.

14. If asked, can your team move as one to get the job done quickly, the answer is yes. Any team when confronted with a common hardship will work together. Even enemies when faced with trouble in the same boat will help each other, just as the left hand helps the right.

15. Teams that establish roots become complacent and unreliable.

16. Properly cross-train the team members to be successful regardless of the situation or environment.

17. Those best at leading a process improvement initiative can lead an entire team as if it were one fully motivated person.

18. The movements of the process improvement leader should be quiet and inconspicuous and his management style fair and structured so as not to be taken lightly.

19. There is no need to let the team members know every thought or plan, best to keep these things from them so they can concentrate on the work at hand.

20. Continually adjust and modify your routine so you don't become predictable.

21. Setting specific achievable goals unifies the team and motivates them to do better and to act as one.

22. The process improvement team must understand the different types of environment and set the appropriate strategy based on the type of resistance expected for each department climate.

23. Building a team and putting it into difficult situations is the job of the process improvement leader. Ability to adapt to unknown or difficult environments and various types of resistance are fundamental requirements of the team members.

24. Teams usually work best when far away from home and get lax when back home. Keep them motivated and learning regardless of where they are or what project or lack of project is at hand so that when a difficult project with a tight deadline comes along they are completely prepared and ready to begin.

25. Those without senior management support and who can't document existing processes can't create a starting point. Those who don't learn the existing workflow can't assign work to the team members properly. Those without existing process resources to provide guidance and knowledge transfer of an existing process are lost. The process improvement team must know all of these things. When the process improvement team tries to begin analyzing they become unorganized and lost with each team member off in a separate direction.

26. Consequently, if you do not get senior management support, do not exude authority and make idle threats, your team becomes vulnerable.

27. Establish authority by dictating policy and issuing rewards that go against the grain and exceed existing policy and your team will act as one.

28. Manage the team as though managing a single person. Assign them tasks with specific goals rather than inspirational speeches. Motivate them with rewards for success rather than punishment for failure.

29. Tell them failure would be catastrophic and they will work hard. Give them a difficult task and they will complete it. When they are working to save their jobs they will reach the desired outcome.

30. The leader's task is to lead with overblown needs and resistance by concentrating on the project regardless of where it is so all resistance is eliminated before the project is formally begun.

31. Once the project formally begins, all thoughts of backing out should be forgotten completely.

32. Any resistance should be immediately escalated to senior management.

33. When a department shows cooperation act fast and gain as much as possible from what they may block

first before they have a chance to become obstructive.

34. Keep the team disciplined to anticipate resistance and to act before it happens. So walk in gently then sprint when you see an opening before anyone can become obstructive.

12. DRASTIC ACTION

1. Be prepared to employ one or a combination of the following as needed

    a) Reorganization of department

    b) Dismissal of staff or managers

    c) Relocating the process which needs improving to another team

    d) Cutting the budget, space or both of offending department

    e) Eliminating tools they employ

2. Ensure you have strong senior management support before venturing to perform any of these actions.

3. Know the proper time to perform these actions. Best sooner rather than later.

a) When able to reorganize do it right away while the opportunity is there.

b) Don't bother reprimanding the staff when the obstruction problem is with management.

4. Learn to adapt to the situation and adjust your strategy accordingly.

5. When taking drastic action, there are five things to consider

a) If the department attempts to reorganize internally, reorganize the entire department right away

b) If you dismiss some managers but there is no change in cooperation, there are other managers present causing dissent

c) Wait for things to settle and work to resume before starting your project

d) When presented with an opportunity for drastic action take it, do not wait for drastic action to happen from within

e) When taking drastic action, do not eliminate the resources you will need to complete your project

6. In every process improvement each of the five components for organizational change should be

known and employed at the proper time should the situation warrant.

7. Reorganization to help a process improvement initiative brings clarity and cooperation.

8. Words can spur some movement but will not overcome obstinate behavior.

9. Reorganization for the sake of change is not good as it may damage team morale.

10. The more successful leader will be the one who plans well and makes progress by encouraging cooperation through rewards and enticements for those who contribute the most.

11. Don't make drastic changes when there is nothing to be gained.

12. Never act out of emotion. Do not make changes out of anger. While your anger may subside, actions taken out of anger cannot be taken back or forgotten.

13. Once reorganization is done and managers dismissed, it cannot be taken back nor the managers brought back to their former positions.

14. There is always a way to manage the situation by proceeding with caution rather than with emotion.

13. PREP WORK AND INFORMATION GATHERING

1. A major process improvement initiative is very disruptive and expensive both in time and money. Larger projects which may take several years to complete will consume resources needed elsewhere and impact productivity.

2. Failure to properly evaluate the conditions, climate for change and required support because of poor planning and lack of information are the signs of a poor leader.

3. Properly preparing for the project is essential and shouldn't be done after the work has started. Knowledge of the environment and conditions must be obtained from among those affected and impacted by the current process to properly determine project strategy.

4. What separates the great process improvement leader from others is the ability to gather all needed information to properly assess the project and formulate a detailed strategy plan.

5. Areas to obtain information from are:

   a) Documented procedures

   b) Detailed process instructions

   c) Affected users of the process

   d) The process owner

   e) Staff within or from the department administering the process

6. Documented procedures are usually instructions given to outside teams to meet compliance requirements but provide little detailed knowledge.

7. Detailed process instructions are the written steps for how the process was intended to be performed.

8. Affected users know the request side of the process and are useful for gathering information regarding problems with the current process.

9. The process owner would supply compliance and corporate requirements for the process.

10. Staff within would know what is truly performed to execute the process.

11. Ensure you reward staff members within the department who provide information. Let it not be known who is providing information.

12. If the information provided secretly comes out in the open then the person who was providing it has been found out and may get fired, reprimanded or reassigned.

13. Be honest and forthright with those providing information in order to gain their trust.

14. Before you can begin a process improvement project, you need to know who the key stakeholders and process owners really are.

15. It is extremely important to know who is feeding you information in order to properly assess the value and accuracy of that information.

16. Those most loyal to the current management must be sought out and converted with the benefits of the project and appreciation of senior management.

17. It is through the help of those most loyal that you are able to garner the support of the staff.

18. They are usually the best ones who can provide and correct miss-information sent to the staff.

19. The purpose of collecting all this information is to properly asset, plan and execute the project. For that reason, those who provide the most help should be properly rewarded.

20. The best process improvement leaders are the ones who accurately collect needed information in order to properly asses the job. Success or failure of the project is dependent on this assessment.

14. BIBLIOGRAPHY

The Art of War by Sun Tzu, translated by Thomas Cleary (1988 edition) Shambhala Publications

The Art of War by Sun Tzu, translated by Lionel Giles, The Project Gutenberg eBook 1994 edition

The Art of War by Sun Tzu, translated by Lionel Giles M.A., Literature Project edition of 1910 translation

The Art of War by Sun Tzu, edited by James Clavell (1983). Delacorte Press.

The Art of War by Sun Tzu, translated by Ralph D. Sawyer (1994).

The Art of War by Sun Tzu, translated by Lionel Giles, Chinese Text Project edition

http://ctext.org/art-of-war

The Art of War by Sun Tzu, translated by J.H. Huang (1993) The New Translation. Quill William Morrow.

Sun Tzu, translated and annotated by Thomas Huynh and the Editors of Sonshi.com (2008).

www.sonshi.com/learn.html